Jesus Has Jumped Highest

FELICIA IFY
ONWUDIWE-CHIDIKE

JESUS HAS JUMPED HIGHEST
Copyright © 2020
FELICIA IFY ONWUDIWE-CHIDIKE

Scripture taken from the New King James Version®. Copyright © 1982 by Thomas Nelson. Used by permission. All rights reserved.

Published by
Faith Revival Ministries International Publishing
London, England

Printed in the UK
Artwork: Admin@thevinemedia.co.uk

All rights reserved under the International Copyright Law. Contents and/or cover may not be reproduced in whole or in part in any form without the express written consent of the publisher

Contents

INTRODUCTION 4

CHAPTER 1
Coronavirus Is Demonic.. 9

CHAPTER 2 19
Love is Reciprocal

CHAPTER 3 25
Love is a Covenant Relationship

CHAPTER 4 35
God Loves the United Kingdom

CHAPTER 5 41
God Speaks To Us In Different Ways

CHAPTER 6 47
Who Was the First Evangelist?

The Book of Visions 57

Jesus Has Jumped Highest

INTRODUCTION

There are two kinds of kingdoms. The first is the Kingdom of God Almighty. This kingdom of God and Jesus Christ His son is full of Love and Light. Everyone who comes to this kingdom learns the process of loving one another because it is the principle that governs the kingdom. Here, when one makes a mistake one repents and confesses it and so is forgiven.

Matthew 18:15-17 NKJV;
"Moreover, if your brother sins against you, go and tell him his fault between you and him alone. If he hears you, you have gained your

brother. But if he will not hear, take with you one or two more, that 'by the mouth of two or three witnesses every word may be established.' And if he refuses to hear them, tell it to the church. But if he refuses even to hear the church, let him be to you like a heathen and a tax collector."

In this Kingdom, no one is allowed to hate anyone. **1 John 3: 15 NKJV** states

"Whoever hates his brother is a murderer, and you know that no murderer has eternal life abiding in him."

The second Kingdom is the kingdom of darkness where Satan and his agents operate from. This is also called darkness because there is no love and is based firmly on the works of the flesh as stated in **Galatians 5:19-21 NKJV;**

"Now the works of the flesh are evident, which are: adultery, fornication, uncleanness, lewdness, idolatry, sorcery, hatred, contentions, jealousies, outbursts of wrath, selfish ambitions,

dissensions, heresies, envy, murders, drunkenness, revelries, and the like; of which I tell you beforehand, just as I also told you in time past, that those who practice such things will not inherit the kingdom of God."

Satan instils fear in the minds of people, they become suspicious of one another, he sows seeds of discord, stress and jealousy. The world is full of negativity and bad characters, but God has given us His spirit of love to dwell with His people. The bible says no evil shall come near us according to **Psalm 91: 9-10 NKJV;**

"Because you have made the Lord, who is my refuge, Even the Most High, your dwelling place, No evil shall befall you, Nor shall any plague come near your dwelling."

Therefore, Coronavirus is an evil plan of the enemy and it shall not devour us.

In **2 Chronicles 20: 20-23** we see clearly the awesomeness and greatness of God. Our God is a powerful God; He holds the whole world in His hands. When you trust in Him, He will take over your battles just like He did with the people of Judah. The only thing we need to do at this time and season is to trust in God, have absolute faith in Him so that we will be delivered from any battle, unpleasant situations, sickness, financial challenges, any problem at all and even this pandemic called coronavirus.

CHAPTER ONE

Corona Virus is Demonic

Many years ago, I saw a vision where some creatures resembling ice cream cones were jumping in competition to know **whose god will jump highest,** then the people standing by started to shout, 'Buddha has jumped highest'. Initially I agreed with the crowd but suddenly I changed my mind and said **"no, Jesus has jumped highest"**. At that same time, I heard a voice that said, **"I will break the yoke"**. I looked back and saw that a big hand had broken a baton that tried to hit me from behind. But the amazing thing was that the baton was broken before the completion of that statement which was in future tense. The Lord reminded me of this vision in the month of February 2020.

The Lord Jesus will use this Pandemic to bring a revival to prove His Lordship; Jesus Christ of Nazareth is the King of all kings and Lord of all lords. God has highly exalted Him and given Him a name above all names that at the mention of His name every knee shall bow, and every tongue confess Him as Lord in Heaven, on earth and under Heaven. *(See **Philippians 2: 9-11**)*

> *For by Him all things were created that are in heaven and that are on earth, visible and invisible, whether thrones or dominions or principalities or powers. All things were created through Him and for Him. And He is before all things, and in Him all things consist. And He is the head of the body, the church, who*

is the beginning, the firstborn from the dead, that in all things He may have the preeminence.

For it pleased the Father that in Him all the fullness should dwell, and by Him to reconcile all things to Himself, by Him, whether things on earth or things in heaven, having made peace through the blood of His cross. Colossians 1:16-20

The Love of God

Jesus died for us because of the love He has for us. He commanded us to love one another as He has loved us. The following passage teaches a valuable lesson here viewing the oil in the text as the **oil of love.**

Matthew 25: 1-13 NKJV;
"Then the kingdom of heaven shall be likened to ten virgins who took their lamps and went out to meet the bridegroom. Now five of them were wise, and five were foolish. Those who were foolish took their lamps and took no oil with them, but the wise took oil in their vessels with their lamps. But while the bridegroom was

delayed, they all slumbered and slept. "And at midnight a cry was heard: 'Behold, the bridegroom is coming; go out to meet him!' Then all those virgins arose and trimmed their lamps. And the foolish said to the wise, 'Give us some of your oil, for our lamps are going out.' But the wise answered, saying, 'No, lest there should not be enough for us and you; but go rather to those who sell, and buy for yourselves.' And while they went to buy, the bridegroom came, and those who were ready went in with him to the wedding; and the door was shut.

"Afterward the other virgins came also, saying, 'Lord, Lord, open to us!' But he answered and said, 'Assuredly, I say to you, I do not know you.' "Watch therefore, for you know neither the day nor the hour in which the Son of Man is coming."

According to **1 John 2: 1- 8**, the one that loves is in the **Light**.

CHAPTER ONE: Corona Virus is Demonic

Antichrist

1 John 2: 18-19 KJV;
"Little children, it is the last time: and as ye have heard that antichrist shall come, even now are there many antichrists; whereby we know that it is the last time. They went out from us, but they were not of us; for if they had been of us, they would no doubt have continued with us: but they went out, that they might be made manifest that they were not all of us."

and **verse 20** says
"But ye have the unction from the Holy One and ye know the truth".

Furthermore, **verses 28-29** reiterate as follows;
"And now, little children, abide in Him, that when He appears, we may have confidence and not be ashamed before Him at His coming. If you know that He is righteous, you know that everyone who practices righteousness is born of Him."

Jesus Christ

Who is Jesus Christ? He is the son of God who was born of a woman and who came to die for mankind on the cross to wash our sins away. He died because of the love He has for us all. This is illustrated perfectly in **John 13: 1-8** where He was preparing for His crucifixion;

"Now before the Feast of the Passover, when Jesus knew that His hour had come that He should depart from this world to the Father, having loved His own who were in the world, He loved them to the end. And supper being ended, the devil having already put it into the heart of Judas Iscariot, Simon's son, to betray Him, Jesus, knowing that the Father had given all things into His hands, and that He had come from God and was going to God, rose from supper and laid aside His garments, took a towel and girded Himself. After that, He poured water into a basin and began to wash the disciples' feet, and to wipe them with the towel with which He was girded. Then He came to Simon Peter. And Peter said to Him, "Lord, are You washing my feet?" Jesus

answered and said to him, "What I am doing you do not understand now, but you will know after this."

Peter said to Him, "You shall never wash my feet!" Jesus answered him, "If I do not wash you, you have no part with Me."

Jesus demonstrated the true meaning of love by washing His disciple's feet.

Also, in verses 34-35; He gave them a new commandment to love one another as He has loved us. By this love shall all men know that ye are my disciples of ye love one another.

Therefore, the DNA for Christians is Love. The DNA for Anti-Christ is the lack of Love.

REFLECTIONS

CHAPTER ONE: Corona Virus is Demonic

Jesus Has Jumped Highest

CHAPTER TWO

Love is Reciprocal

It is a two-way street, love one another. Anyone that believes in Christ must obey His commandments which includes loving. When you love someone, you think good of the person, if the person does wrong, you will correct him/her with brotherly love.

A kingdom that is divided against itself cannot stand; the church as a whole is the kingdom of God. God is the creator and owner of the world which is the kingdom and has made us children of the kingdom. It does not matter which church you attend or denomination you belong to; we are still one body. The Lord told me many years ago that those who despise Christians from other churches apart from theirs are many but are in darkness, while those who accept other Christians regardless of personal beliefs are few but are in the light. **<u>Discrimination</u> is not of God.** The important thing about being a Christian is receiving Christ Jesus as our Lord and Saviour and this will bring forth the fruit of love for one another (See **1 Corinthians 12:11-31**)

Verses 12 – 14 NKJV state;

"For as the body is one and has many members, but all the members of that one body, being many, are one body, so also is Christ. For by one Spirit we were all baptized into one body—whether Jews or Greeks, whether slaves or free—and have all been made to drink into one Spirit. For in fact the body is not one member but many."

Also, **1 Corinthians 13:13 NKJV** the word of God emphasises the greatest gift of all;

"And now abide faith, hope, love, these three; ***but the greatest of these is love.***"

Agape, love DNA from Christ Jesus

Jesus Christ is created from Love, everything about Him consists of Love. He was created because of love and this love for humanity drove Him to the cross. He died for us because He loved us, even the gospel is love. Again, **John 13: 34 – 35 NKJV** instructs;

"A new commandment I give to you, that you love one another; as I have loved you, that you also love one another. By this all will know that you are My disciples, if you have love for one another."

God so loved Abraham because Abraham loved even to the point where he was willing to sacrifice his only son Isaac because he believed God who gave Isaac to him can equally raise him up from the dead. This difficult but simple act was counted to Abraham as righteousness. Abraham loved God and obeyed Him. (See **Genesis 22:1-19**)

The love for God makes one obey His voice and so there must be a relationship before one can hear or recognise God's voice.

> **Hebrews 4:7**[b] *"Today, if you will hear His voice, do not harden your hearts."*

It is very essential to communicate with someone who is close to you. Communication is a two-way street, one talks, and the other listens. David is another example of a person who was close to God in the Bible. See to **2 Samuel 22** where David praised God for his deliverance through song before he became king because he was assured that God will deliver him.

REFLECTIONS

Jesus Has Jumped Highest

CHAPTER THREE

Love is a Covenant Relationship

God entered into a covenant relationship with Abraham. **Genesis 22:16-19 NKJV;**

"By Myself I have sworn, says the Lord, because you have done this thing, and have not

withheld your son, your only son—blessing I will bless you and multiplying I will multiply your descendants as the stars of the heaven and as the sand which is on the seashore; and your descendants shall possess the gate of their enemies. In your seed all the nations of the earth shall be blessed, because you have obeyed My voice." So Abraham returned to his young men, and they rose and went together to Beersheba; and Abraham dwelt at Beersheba."

A covenant is a binding agreement usually between two people: in the days of the bible, it was often made between God and man. Abraham believed God's promise to him and it was counted for him as righteousness; **Galatians 3:6**. When you are in a covenant relationship with God, God speaks to you about His plans and purposes. Your part is to listen to His voice and obey.

Genesis 17: 1-27, narrates how God entered into a covenant relationship with Abraham.

CHAPTER THREE: Love is a Covenant Relationship

The Sign of the Covenant

Genesis 17:1-3 NKJV;

"When Abram was ninety-nine years old, the Lord appeared to Abram and said to him, "I am Almighty God; walk before Me and be blameless. And I will make My covenant between Me and you and will multiply you exceedingly." Then Abram fell on his face, and God talked with him…"

The conversation between God and Abraham in the following verses is a long one, where He clearly sets out the plans for Abraham's future with promises and assurances based on specific instructions. The relationship between God and Abraham was so deep that they spoke back and forth so much so that in **Genesis 18**, Abraham pleaded repeatedly with God for Sodom and God listened to him all the way until **verse 33** which recorded the end of that conversation.

Abraham did intercede for Sodom, **Genesis 18: 33 NKJV;**

> *"So the Lord went His way as soon as He had finished speaking with Abraham; and Abraham returned to his place".*

If Abraham had continued to ask for one righteous person God would have listened to him, but he stopped at 10 persons.

An Intercessor

An intercessor is a 'go – between' between God and man and are prophetic as well in their calling. They hear from God and intercede on behalf of man. Either men or women can be intercessors.

Abram considered Sarai a covenant partner even though she pressed him to have relations with her maid which later resulted in her pain in **Genesis 16: 4-6**. God protects the interest of His covenant children even when they make mistakes out of fear.

CHAPTER THREE: Love is a Covenant Relationship

Genesis 20: 1-6 NKJV;

"And Abraham journeyed from there to the South, and dwelt between Kadesh and Shur, and stayed in Gerar. Now Abraham said of Sarah his wife, "She is my sister." And Abimelech king of Gerar sent and took Sarah. But God came to Abimelech in a dream by night, and said to him, "Indeed you are a dead man because of the woman whom you have taken, for she is a man's wife." But Abimelech had not come near her; and he said, "Lord, will You slay a righteous nation also? Did he not say to me, 'She is my sister'? And she, even she herself said, 'He is my brother.' In the integrity of my heart and innocence of my hands I have done this." And God said to him in a dream, "Yes, I know that you did this in the integrity of your heart. For I also withheld you from sinning against Me; therefore I did not let you touch her."

In **verse 7**, God told Abimelech that Abraham is a prophet, which allows him as a prophet to pray for Abimelech.

> *"Now therefore, restore the man's wife; for he is a prophet, and he will pray for you and you shall live. But if you do not restore her, know that you shall surely die, you and all who are yours."*

Covenant relationships matter a great deal to God and the important thing is to obey God's voice when He speaks. It is very vital to obey His voice; God does not tolerate disobedience. Even as meek as Moses was, God did not tolerate his disobedience after God asked him to speak to the rock, but he struck the rock instead. God expected him to have obeyed His instruction.

Jesus our Saviour and Redeemer had a covenant relationship with God the Father before He came to earth to redeem us. **Luke 4:18-21 NKJV;**

> *"The Spirit of the Lord is upon Me,*
> *Because He has anointed Me*
> *To preach the gospel to the poor;*
> *He has sent Me to heal the broken-hearted,*
> *To proclaim liberty to the captives*
> *And recovery of sight to the blind,*
> *To set at liberty those who are oppressed;*
> *To proclaim the acceptable year of the Lord."*

CHAPTER THREE: Love is a Covenant Relationship

Then He closed the book and gave it back to the attendant and sat down. And the eyes of all who were in the synagogue were fixed on Him.

And He began to say to them, "Today this Scripture is fulfilled in your hearing."

Jesus understood the covenant He had with God, and He was determined to carry out His covenant assignment. **Hebrews 10:6-7 NKJV;**

"In burnt offerings and sacrifices for sin
You had no pleasure.
Then I said, 'Behold, I have come
In the volume of the book it is written of Me
To do Your will, O God.'"

Verses 24 and 25 of the same chapter, show that Jesus has purified us by His blood and encourages us to exhort one another and to love.

"*And let us consider one another in order to stir up love and good works not forsaking the assembling of ourselves together, as is the manner of some, but exhorting one another, and so much the more as you see the Day approaching."*

Jesus remembered His covenant partners just as He has remembered United Kingdom and instructed them to come out of Europe. **<u>Brexit is of God.</u>**

REFLECTIONS

Jesus Has Jumped Highest

CHAPTER FOUR

God Loves the United Kingdom

Brexit is of God; He has spoken since 1990 about Brexit. God said He will bless the UK because of her forefathers who served God in such an honest way and travelled all over the world to spread the good news about Jesus Christ. (see the preface).

God will use the UK to provoke other European countries unto righteousness. There is a revival that will hit England whilst God is restoring back her former glory. We must be strong and continue our lives as normal as He supports us through this transition. It is not about the power of the Dollar, pound Sterling or Euro, but the **mighty power of God within us all.**

God's Perfect will for Mankind

In the beginning, God created man (Adam) and woman (Eve) to worship Him, in total love and unity. With this love and unity for one another they will give birth to children of their own kind, who will love each other as well with honesty and respect to God in obedience to God's commandments and intentions. **Genesis 2:4-25.**

Observe: God created everything mankind needs in order to live a wonderful, peaceful and blissful life before He created man. He gave Adam authority to name everything that He had created. **Verses 19-20.**

Why did God allow Adam to name everything He (God)

had created? Because He loved Adam; who represents mankind. Love is reciprocal. For love to be effective it must be given and received. God created man (Adam) and Eve (Woman) to love themselves without partiality. In return, they must obey God with all their heart and mind. It was supposed to be a cordial relationship, but Satan the devil came and deceived Eve to eat the fruit from the forbidden tree, that God warned them never to touch. That tree was the tree of KNOWLEDGE.

Inter-dependence

God's intention is for man to depend completely on Him (the Creator) for man's entire life and subsistence. The tree of knowledge that God asked Adam and Eve not to eat from was the tree of good and evil.

Genesis 2:16-17 NIV;
"And the Lord God commanded the man, "you are free to eat from any tree in the garden: but you must not eat from the tree of the knowledge of good and evil, for when you eat from it you certainly die".

This clearly means human beings must depend on God to direct us on our path. How can we depend on God? We can do this by searching for God's approval through prayers. This is exactly what Jesus said when He came to earth to die in order to save us: **Genesis 1:27-28 NIV;**

> *"So God created mankind in His own image, in the image of God He created them, male and female he created them. God blessed them and said to them," Be fruitful and increase in number, fill the earth and subdue it. Rule over the fish in the sea and the birds in the sky and over every living creature that moves on the ground."*

The first 'Adam' disobeyed God's instruction and obeyed Satan; but the last 'Adam'- Jesus Christ – came down from heaven to redeem man from the punishment man incurred for this disobedience. The last Adam - Jesus Christ – obeyed God's commandment even unto death.

Now that Jesus has redeemed human beings back to God our Father and Creator; we must depend on God solely, for us to live a Godly life.

… CHAPTER FOUR: God Loves the United Kingdom

REFLECTIONS

Jesus Has Jumped Highest

CHAPTER FIVE

God Speaks To Us In Different Ways

A) **Dreams:** God can show us things through dreams whilst we are sleeping.

B) **Visions:** God can show us things supernaturally, visions take place when we are awake. The word of God is the Bible and the Holy Spirit reminds us of the words of the Bible in order to confirm what He has in mind for us.

Prophecy

No prophecy of the scripture is of any private interpretation. **2 Peter 1:20-21 NIV:**

" Above all, you must understand that no prophecy of scripture came about by the prophet's own interpretation of things, For prophecy never had its origin in the human will, but prophets (though human); spoke from God as they were carried along by the Holy Spirit."

For further reference, **2 Peter 1:16-19 NIV**;

"For we did not follow cleverly devised stories when we told you about the coming of our Lord Jesus Christ in power, but we were eyewitnesses of His majesty. He received honour and glory form God the Father when the voice came to Him from the Majesty Glory, saying, "This is my Son, whom I love; with him I am well pleased". We ourselves heard this

CHAPTER FIVE: God Speaks To Us In Different Ways

voice that came from heaven when we were with him on the sacred mountain. We also have the prophetic message as something completely reliable and you will do well to pay attention to it, as to a light shining in a dark place, until the day dawns and the morning star rises in your hearts."

Other examples of the prophecies within this book include:
- God's revelation that Tony Blair would win the 1997 election
- The recent incident in Zimbabwe was also revealed by God in 1990.

Conclusion

Prophetic Utterance

God is restoring His covenant relationship with mankind. He has a plan and purpose for creating us no matter the gender, age or colour, what matters is your relationship with God. **Romans 9:10-18**

Prophecy about Zimbabwe

In 1994, God showed me a vision where President Robert Mugabe sat at a conference table with three other black leaders discussing with no paper or pen, which means no agenda. God then asked me to go to Zimbabwe and tell the President about the vision. That time I had a Nigerian passport and so I went to Zimbabwe house to obtain a visa to travel.

When I got here, the secretary asked me where in Zimbabwe, I was going, I asked her what's the capital called? She said Harare, I said write Harare there and then she asked where in Harare, I said, write any town. At this point, she inquired who I was, and I proceeded to tell her about the vision. She connected me to women fellowship, and I wrote to them. My letter reached Dr Regina Galla, the younger sister of Robert Mugabe and she connected me to her brother.

When I got to Zimbabwe, the President invited me to his presidential palace. I narrated the vision to him. He said "who am 1 to argue with God and that he would tell his party members. I was planning to go back to see him when I heard that women and children were still not taken care of; God will restore Zimbabwe when they embark on taking care of women and children.

CHAPTER FIVE: God Speaks To Us In Different Ways

REFLECTIONS

Jesus Has Jumped Highest

CHAPTER SIX

Who Was the First Evangelist?

In mid-summer 1990, I knelt down to study the book of Jonah Chapter 3, As I read on, I heard a voice say to me: *"Write down the verses that have blessed your spirit"*. I answered "write down? Why?" He said, *"you will preach on it today."*

In July 1990, our ministry Dynamic Gospel Ministries International was launched as an evangelical outreach. We invited a Bishop from Nigeria, Africa to be our guest speaker. As at that time, we had no members at all except for my husband, who is called Pastor Joe, myself and our two young children; Tochukwu was 6 years old and Chinwe was 1 year and 9 months.

The town I am from originally is called Dikenafai in Imo State of Nigeria. When I was growing up in that town, it was an accepted norm that women were meant to be seen and not to be heard. I was taught to speak through my husband, I was raised to believe that was the custom and I acted accordingly up until July 1990. Surely, we had our fair share of quarrels as any married couple would but never did we allow it to happen in public. That was my conception about the life of a woman.

Therefore, when the Holy Spirit told me that I would preach Jonah Chapter 3 in the crusade Pastor Joe and I organised, I said, "No Lord, it is not possible". I said to Him; "Lord why do you want to damage my reputation? People will say that I have come to take

CHAPTER SIX: Who Was the First Evangelist?

over the ministry from my husband. Besides, our guest speaker is from Africa". I went on to tell Him that I am already having problems believing that we should go into ministry work and He was compounding the problem. Then He asked me: *"WHO WAS THE FIRST EVANGELIST?"* I answered *"MARY MAGDALENE"*. He said to me: "If I could ask a woman to go tell her brethren that I have risen from the dead, what else can you preach apart from Jesus being crucified and risen?" I then replied, *"Alright Lord, I will do so"*. This was confirmed for me in **Mark 16:1-11 NKJV where.**

"Now when the Sabbath was past, Mary Magdalene, Mary the mother of James, and Salome bought spices, that they might come and anoint Him. Very early in the morning, on the first day of the week, they came to the tomb when the sun had risen. And they said among themselves, "Who will roll away the stone from the door of the tomb for us?" But when they looked up, they saw that the stone had been rolled away—for it was very large. And entering the tomb, they saw a young man clothed in a long white robe sitting on the right side; and they were alarmed.

But he said to them, "Do not be alarmed. You seek Jesus of Nazareth, who was crucified. He is risen! He is not here. See the place where they laid Him. But go, tell His disciples—and Peter—that He is going before you into Galilee; there you will see Him, as He said to you."

So they went out quickly and fled from the tomb, for they trembled and were amazed. And they said nothing to anyone, for they were afraid. Now when He rose early on the first day of the week, He appeared first to Mary Magdalene, out of whom He had cast seven demons. She went and told those who had been with Him, as they mourned and wept. And when they heard that He was alive and had been seen by her, they did not believe."

I drew a lot of encouragement after I read this scripture. I was also challenged by **verse 2**, which says that these women came to the sepulchre very early in the morning; this denotes determination and first priority. Anyone that determines to honour God with their first fruit would also get God's first blessing irrespective of

CHAPTER SIX: Who Was the First Evangelist?

sex, colour or race. The Bible in **Matthew 6:33 KJV** clearly says: *"But seek ye first the kingdom of God and His righteousness; and all these things shall be added unto you".*

Everything Has Been Prepared but People Are Making Excuses

When the Lord appeared to me in 1987, He opened His palms and I saw the nail prints. I began to scream; "Lord You are real! So, You are real!" I said to Him, "Could You please show Yourself to other Christians so they too will know that You are real?". But He said to me: *"Note that it is like the parable of the marriage feast that everything has been prepared but people are making excuses".*

The Word of God is so precious and expensive that God will not give it or talk to people with laissez-faire attitudes. He will not give the children's food to the dogs. God delights in people who appreciate Him as the Almighty God, and those who will not forget where He brought them out from. This Mary Magdalene did not forget the day that Jesus cast out seven demons from her. **Verse 9** reminds us of that account. She appreciated what the Lord did for her and did not care about the accusations they labelled against Jesus. As far as she was concerned, Jesus was the best of the best. In **Matthew 16:13-15 NKJV,** the Bible records;

"When Jesus came into the region of Caesarea Philippi, He asked His disciples, saying, "Who do men say that I, the Son of Man, am?" So they said, "Some say John the Baptist, some Elijah, and others Jeremiah or one of the prophets." He said to them, "But who do you say that I am?"

The pertinent question there is who do you think Jesus is? It does not matter who people think you are; It does not matter whether Pope, Bishop, Apostle, Reverend, Elder, Deacon or whoever else thinks that God cannot use you as a vessel because you are a woman, or because of your race, background etc. What matters is, who do you think Jesus is? Are you sure of your calling? Do you know who has called you? Do you remember what He said to you when He called you? Then stay faithful to that calling.

Matthew 16: 16-18 NKJV;

"Simon Peter answered and said, "You are the Christ, the Son of the living God." Jesus answered and said to him, "Blessed are you, Simon Bar-Jonah, for flesh and blood has not revealed this to you, but My Father who is in heaven. And I also say to you that you are Peter, and on this rock, I will build My church, and the gates of Hades shall not prevail against it."

REFLECTIONS

CHAPTER SIX: Who Was the First Evangelist?

Book of Visions

Vision About Nigeria

In 2011, the Lord told me that He will appoint a president to Nigeria, who will depend solely on Him, He will use him to transform the economy to the point of One British Pound Sterling (£) being equal to six Nigerian Naira (₦) but God did not tell me who the president would be or when this will happen.

In the vision God showed me, I was praying, then suddenly I realised I was singing this **song:**
Reign in me.........x2
Sovereign Lord ....
Reign in me..............x2
Sovereign Lord ....
Reign in me......................
Captivate my heart............
Let thy kingdom come.......x2.
Establish here your throne..................
Let thine will be done........................x2
Jesus reign in me..........................
sovereign Lord reign in me..........

Then I saw a big hall with a large number of people where an elderly white man lifted a prayer book and declared '*if you have not interceded for Nigeria in 4 years then go!*' Suddenly and without question or argument, about 75% of the crowd left. As I was wondering what that meant, I saw freshly cooked rice and then someone brought in old rice in a tiny old bowl. This same elderly white man refused the mixture and said, '*you cannot mix the old rice with the new one*'. The Lord encouraged me to publish this vision in a

Nigerian newspaper. As usual I asked Him for a confirmation, and He gave me **Galatians 3:9 NKJV;** *"So then those who are of faith are blessed with believing Abraham."*

I went ahead and published it in Vanguard Newspaper on the 13th of March 2015 before the actual election. Then God asked me to republish it and so on the 22nd of January 2018, it was published again in The Vanguard newspaper. Therefore, the re-election was from God.

There is a revival that will soon hit the whole world, God will restore things as He Has purposed in His Heart. Love for each other will be restored as He has commanded us.

According to **Jeremiah 31:33-34 NKJV;**
"But this is the covenant that I will make with the house of Israel after those days, says the Lord: I will put My law in their minds, and write it on their hearts; and I will be their God, and they shall be My people. No more shall every man teach his neighbour, and every man his brother, saying, 'Know the Lord,' for they

all shall know Me, from the least of them to the greatest of them, says the Lord. For I will forgive their iniquity, and their sin I will remember no more."

See also **Isaiah 62.**

Likewise **Hebrews 10:16 NKJV** declares:
"This is the covenant that I will make with them after those days, says the Lord: I will put My laws into their hearts, and in their minds, I will write them,"

The vision for Brazil

Many years ago, God showed me a vision about Brazil. I saw an image with the face of a human being and the body of a tree. Then God said to me that the image is the spirit that hinders revival in Brazil and that I should pray against it. Years later I heard that there was a revival in Brazil. That revival will continue in Jesus name.

The vision about America

In the year 2016, God showed me a vision where Trump walked down to Hilary Clinton and they were looking at each other eyeball to eyeball. After that I saw some stains on his shirt and God told me to wipe it, so his call to be president is of God. The blessing of God makes rich and adds no sorrow.

Finally brethren, let us love one another as He has commanded us, it is love amongst ourselves that will bring this revival. Stay reminded of the words of Christ in **John chapter 13: 34-35 NKJV,** Jesus said to His disciples *"A new commandment I give to you, that you love one another; as I have loved you, that you also love one another. By this all will know that you are My disciples, if you have love for one another."*

In case you desire to be empowered by God or get closer to God, repeat this prayer:

> Dear Father in Heaven. I desire to know you more; I believe in my heart that Jesus Christ is the son of God. I believe He came to earth to die for my sins. He was crucified on the cross to pay for my debt. He rose from the dead on the third day and ascended to heaven. I confess with my mouth the Lordship of Jesus. Forgive me for my ignorance today, I confess Jesus Christ as my Lord and Saviour.

Thank You Father in heaven; in Jesus Name. Amen
Romans 10:8-11

REFLECTIONS

Jesus Has Jumped Highest